purrles of feline wisdom

by BOB LOVKA

Photographs by Alan & Sandy Carey

BOWTIE PRESS®

Irvine, California

Nick Clemente, Special Consultant
Karla Austin, Project Manager
Ruth Strother, Editor-at-Large
Michelle Martinez, Editor
Lisa Barfield, Designer

Library of Congress Control Number: 2003102989

BowTie Press®
A Division of Bowtie, Inc.
3 Burroughs
Irvine, California 92618
Printed and Bound in Singapore
10 9 8 7 6 5 4 3

introduction

It's said that "You can learn a lot just by watching," and if you're watching a feline there's usually more than what meets the eye. Cats seem to belong to a mystical "other world" that coexists with our own. Maybe they're here to translate the messages and advice that their "other world" sends out about how to live, how to love, and how to quit messing things up. Life isn't really all that complicated, but you know how humans are—they never listen!

Fortunately, this little book can help by alerting you to the sights and sounds that cats are telling you—and they're telling you plenty! Cats get their great knowledge and oh-so-simple advice from the teachings of their renowned spiritual guide: The Mew Guru, a singularly brilliant feline who seems to know what makes things tick. The advice from this "Mews," contained herein and communicated through feline companions, may prove to be a catalyst for a less stressful and more enjoyable life—maybe even nine of them.

read on...

You Can't Get Going Until You Start

All big thinkers have grand plans and great dreams, but if you're going to build a better mousetrap, you need to think big, have a goal, and, most importantly, implement the plan! You have to take a paws-on approach to achieve your dream.

Nobody's *purrfect* and nobody gets through life completely on their own. There's no shame in accepting some help along the way.

We All Need
a Little
Helping Hand
Now and Then

Check Out Life's Changes and Get to Know What's New

Curiosity is a good thing! It expands your knowledge and broadens your world. Be alert and aware of what surrounds you. The more you observe, the more interesting things become.

You have been given what it takes to get to the top. Use your gifts to reach your potential! Some felines are bigger and some are smarter, but no one can stop your determination. You're the master of you!

You Are the Master of Your Domain!

Seek...and Be Open to What You Find

The journey you take is going to be filled with twists, turns, stops, and dead ends. The trick is to take it all in stride, to keep pressing forward, and to learn to adapt, adjust, and apply yourself. Your journey will be worth the effort and can take you to places you never expected to go.

You truly belong anywhere! You can make any place your home. For those who express all the facets of their heart and soul there's no such thing as not fitting in. Whether you're a Manx, tabby, calico, or Cheshire cat, you're part of the whole kittenkaboodle that connects us all.

Fit Into Your Surroundings

Sometimes You're
Better Off
Following the Rules

Independence and self-determination are wonderful quali-
ties, but don't ignore the obvious, or the tried and true, just
to assert yourself or have it your own way. Sometimes the "no"
you receive *knows* better than you.

Peace of mind is related to peace in living. You don't have to run after glamorous possessions and gewgaws, the biggest and the best, or the newest and the most to feel fulfilled. The more you own, the more you are owned.

You'll Do Better If You Simplify Your Life

Explore and Learn

Take an interest in all that's around you! A healthy curiosity is the beginning of discovery, which leads to knowledge—the key to wisdom and understanding.

Although you may resemble many others on the outside, on the inside you are one-of-a-kind. Be true to yourself, and if the world tries to label you don't take it to heart. Remember, you're not a simple "this" or a well-defined "that" and certainly not "one of those."

Don't Let the World Label You

Sometimes It Takes a Leap of Faith

Great achievements and success usually involve taking a risk. Anyone can settle for the mediocre, but if you dream big, you have to take some positive action toward your dream. The application of your determination is what counts. Make your leap of faith!

All nine of our lives are happier when we watch out for one another. Treat others as you wish to be treated. You may not have met them all yet, but SVOs (Special Valued Others) are present in your life—cherish them!

Take Good Care of Your Partner

Thank Someone

It's a basic necessity to feel loved and appreciated. One of the most beneficial things to do for others is to acknowledge them for who they are and to thank them for bringing support, help, and happiness to your own nine lives.

Evaluate! Take a look at yourself and see if you're being the cat you've always wanted to be. It's easy to wander off your path if you don't take stock and reset your bearings once in a while. If you don't like what you see, it's time to make some changes.

Take a Good Look at Yourself Every So Often

You Can Never Leave the One You Truly Love Behind

There are at least 1,513 loves that will cross your nine lives but only one who's meant for you. If you ever leave that love it will remain forever on the fringes of your mind and in the deepest recesses of your heart. Hold on to the love of your life!

When you're in love flowers smell sweeter and music moves you to dance. Whether it's a Minute Waltz, an unfinished symphony, or a partner who eventually steps on your paws — to boogie to the best of life's rhythms takes two!

To Dance You Need a Partner

It Doesn't Take Much to Make You Happy

Expensive toys to play with? Catnip to relax? Gourmet choice cuts for every dinner? Who needs it! If you can't be content with all that's provided to you, the things you try to add won't make you happy either.

A world with nine lives offers much to see, so there's a temptation to take things for granted and think you know it all at first glance. Explore life's subtle differences, and you will find in them much worth knowing.

Most Things Require a Closer Inspection

Indulge the Playfulness Within

The world needs more innocent fun! Instead of giving in to a sourpuss attitude and keeping your nose to the grindstone for too long, see the silly inside the mundane. Cultivate the kitten within and take a look at things from a whole new perspective!

The essence of a soul mate is someone who shares your secrets and knows exactly what you mean without having to say a word. This individual isn't a twin or a copycat but someone who's nearly another you. A soul mate helps you keep your soul alive.

Find Your Soul Mate

Don't Get Jangled Up in the Politics of the Situation!

There are those who act catty over absolutely nothing! Dealing with jealousy, favoritism, criticism, cliques, and choosing sides only traps you in a web. By sticking with your individuality, integrity, and sense of what's right, you'll always stand tall.

When you find that your direction, your beliefs, or your situation no longer serves your present needs be flexible and not afraid to change. As you grow, you change, so it's important to shed the things that can't grow with you in order to fit into what is coming ahead.

Shed the Coat That No Longer Fits

Trust Yourself!

If your heart is telling you to take a chance, never fear venturing beyond your norm. You can't land on the other side if you don't jump over the fence! Take heart—you are resilient and will land on your feet. Believe in yourself and be on your way!

An active imagination provides a vacation from everyday reality! It enables you to find new uses for the same old thing and leads you to discover connections, combinations, and correlations between things you never thought had anything to do with one another.

Use Your Imagination!

Face Your Fears

Not dealing with your fears of change, commitment, or chal-
lenges only allows them to grow more ominous. It's tough for
a scaredy-cat to live one life, let alone nine! Think logically, not
emotionally, and you'll discover what can be done to overcome
the situation.

Every individual is unique and has something different to share. Be careful not to get so wrapped up in your own importance that you disregard the views of others. Only by seeing beyond yourself can you understand the whole picture.

See Beyond Yourself

Taste the Moment!

Tomorrow's tuna may be delayed, so enjoy the catfish of the moment. If you're alert and responsive to the here and now, you'll seldom miss a thing. Enjoy today— it can't ever be repeated.

Everyone makes mistakes, but once one is made don't compound the situation by stubbornly pressing on in the same direction. You'll only get stuck further out on a limb. Learn your lesson and take immediate steps to correct things.

In a Losing Situation, Don't Lose the Lesson

Improvise! You Don't Have
to Accept Things the Way They Are

Looking and seeing are two different things. When you look, you're aware of only one dimension—what's easily understood. When you see, you discover new possibilities and can create something marvelous out of the mundane. It makes for a whole new world!

You are an amazing collection of cells, capable of just about anything—good or bad! Respect the world and others in it. Doing the right thing by maintaining your dignity without being arrogant gives you a reason to be proud of your life.

Do It All With a Sense of Dignity

BOB LOVKA is a Southern California-based writer whose work includes poetry, satire, humor books, television, script, and stage show writing. Bob's connection to felines and canines keeps expanding. Homeless cats and dogs look him up constantly and have increased their appearances since Bob wrote *Advice from the Doggy Lama*, *Cat Blessings*, *Dog Blessings*, *The Splendid Little Book of All Things Cat*, *The Splendid Little Book of All Things Dog*, *Cat's Rule!*, *Dog's Rule!*, *Cat's Are Better Than Dogs*, and *Dogs Are Better Than Cats*. Bob is owned by a cat and is tormented by a jealous Lhasa apso.

ALAN & SANDY CAREY have been wildlife and nature photographers for more than twenty years. Their love for nature has taken them all over the world. Their work has appeared in *National Geographic*, *Smithsonian*, *Life*, *Readers Digest*, *Audubon*, *National Wildlife*, and *Time* magazines. When asked what their favorite animal is, their answer is an enthusiastic, "Whatever we are photographing today!" You can also find their work on postcards, billboards, and even on some of the tail sections of Frontier airplanes.